HISTORIC
BRITAIN

CROWN BOOKS

Published in Great Britain 1985 by Crown Books.
CLB 936
Crown Books is a registered imprint of Colour Library Books Ltd.
© 1985 Illustrations and text: Colour Library Books Ltd.,
    Guildford, Surrey, England.
Display and text filmsetting by Acesetters Ltd.,
    Richmond, Surrey, England.
Produced by AGSA, in Barcelona, Spain.
Printed and bound in Barcelona, Spain by Rieusset and Eurobinder.
ISBN 0 86283 317 5

Britain is one of the most beautiful and varied countries in the world. There are towering, forbidding mountains and gentle, rolling hills; wave-lashed cliffs and quiet lakes. But no matter what the scene, it has experienced some ten millennia of human habitation. Throughout Britain man has made his mark, turning a wild and untamed land into a beautiful and civilised nation.

Even the majestic Highlands of Scotland are not free from the hand of man. Windswept glens which have run with blood from ancient clan feuds, now echo to the bleat of sheep. Imported from other regions, the sheep keep down the native flora and impose the short grass upon the hills. The same unnatural landscape has been forced by man upon the lovely slopes of the Lake District. The forests which once covered the crags and sweeping hills of Cumbria were cleared centuries ago for pasture. Today, even the waters of the lakes are disturbed as dozens of colourful craft ply their surfaces.

Around the Wash, beneath the towers of Ely and the spires of Peterborough, spreads one of the most altered landscapes in Britain. There were once over a thousand square miles of marsh in this corner of Britain: marsh so thick and treacherous that Hereward the Wake could hide an army from the might of the Normans for years on end. But beneath the waterlogged morass was the rich, peaty fenland soil, just waiting to be farmed. Since the wild days of Hereward, thousands of men have slaved ceaselessly to dig ditches and drain the fens. Today, the land is among the most productive in Britain. As the farmland reaches, featureless, to the horizon, the wet ditches and clanking pumps are the only reminders of the past.

In South Wales the lovely, green valleys of the prosperous medieval farmer became, in the last century, even more prosperous, but far less beautiful. The coal mining that brought people and wealth to the valleys left behind glowering slag heaps that have drastically changed the valleys.

But even where the impact has not been as great as in the mountains, fens or valleys, the landscape of Britain shows the marks of man. Fields are lined by hedges too straight for nature to have planted them. Meadows are planted with waving grain where once dense forest echoed to the bellows of the deer and the snuffle of the boars. Amongst these artificial fields are the shattered remains of times long past. On barren moors stand lonely stones. The megaliths of Stonehenge are reminders of a long-dead religion that held sway over Britain thousands of years ago. On many a hilltop throughout the islands there is a reminder of less distant days. Gaunt towers and turrets, which are now roofless and silent, mark the homes of warlords who once led their men out to fight in wars now forgotten.

All around are the changes that man has wrought on the land of Britain, but by far the most enduring are his towns. Scattered across the face of the land are many clusters of houses. Each town has its own distinctive character, yet each is the work of the British people. There are small, stone-built towns in the Western Isles that huddle around storm-lashed harbours, waiting for the fishermen to return from the seas. There are grey towns built on the slopes of the Yorkshire Dales that pulse to the beat of the hill-farming around them. In the lowlands, where the wind caresses the waving corn, stand gentler towns. Grouped around the exquisite church steeples, whose bells have chimed the hours for centuries, the towns of the plains rest in tranquillity. The shops and market stalls hum with the babble of voices as one season slips easily into another. The towns of Britain reflect the power man has over the land, but also the way the land can affect the men that live there.

Then there are the cities that owe nothing to their surroundings. The intricate architecture of scholarly Cambridge and Oxford is totally divorced from the lush fields that surround it. The spires and courts are the products of a centuries-old tradition of learning and refinement. London is the result of a long history of trade and commerce. The capital city is such a sprawling mass that its citizens could live for years without seeing the wealth and beauty of the rural landscape beyond the suburbs. But they have built an equally beautiful townscape in which to live. Magnificent examples of architecture, both old and new, crowd the skyline. The classical dome of St Paul's vies with the gleaming Nat. West. Building and the squat bulk of the Tower for the prize of the city's finest edifice.

Whatever the view of Britain, it is one of a land built by man. The ordered fields of Kent are no less artificial than the stone-paved streets of London, the grass-covered glen no more natural than the castle that crowns it. The British people have taken a prodigy of Nature's work and wrought it into the most graceful land on earth.

In the earliest days of Cambridge University the students had to find lodgings wherever they could, but before long colleges began to be founded to house the growing numbers of students. Trinity College (above) was founded by King Henry VIII in 1546. Emmanuel College (below) dates to 1584, while King's College (top right) was founded by Henry VI over a century earlier. The buildings of Clare College (right) are seventeenth century in origin. (Facing page): (top left) Neville's Court, Trinity College, (bottom left) Christ's College, (top right) the bridge of Trinity College, (centre right) King's College and (bottom right) Trinity Hall. (Bottom right) the Senate House and the Old Schools.

The enchanting landscape of England is perhaps at its most dreamlike when the first, light falls of snow lend a fairytale atmosphere to the trees and fields (these pages).

The Lake District is one of the most dramatic and impressive areas of England. It was along the shores of such lakes as Grasmere (left) and in the shadows of mountains like Crinkle Crags and Blowfell (right and below) that Wordsworth penned his immortal lines. His home for nine years, Dove Cottage, stands at the southern end of Grasmere and he was buried in the churchyard of St Oswald's. It was also across this majestic landscape that the redoubtable John Peel hunted. Immortalised in song by a friend, this remarkable man had a lifelong passion for hunting and he kept a pack of dogs so that he could tramp the hills with them whenever he wished.

11

The south coast of England is dotted with dozens of harbours that shelter the small ships in which the English love to put to sea. Each port has its own character and role. Polperro (far right), in Cornwall, once made a very lucrative business out of smuggling, but it is now given over to tourists who come to see this pretty village. Cadgwith (right), in the same county, still relies on fishing. The harbour at Lymington (above and facing page, top), in Hampshire, is a popular refuge for pleasure yachts. It is also the mainland docking point of a car ferry that crosses to Yarmouth (below) on the Isle of Wight. The town, which was sacked by the French in 1524, has not only a fine harbour, but also a sandy beach. Weymouth (facing page, bottom), in Dorset, is also known for its safe, sandy beaches and yacht harbour. The port operates Sealink ferries to the Channel Islands.

13

14

William Shakespeare, perhaps the greatest writer of all time, was married in 1582 to Anne Hathaway, who lived in this beautiful farmhouse about a mile from Stratford-upon-Avon, Warwickshire. It was probably here that the teenage William came to court his future wife, who would appear to have been a few years older than himself. Within a year of the marriage a daughter, Susanna, was born. Shakespeare's later success in London brought prosperity and the family soon moved to a fine house in Stratford.

Thatch has long been an important roofing material in rural England. Even today fine examples of the thatcher's art can be seen throughout the land. (Above) in Welford-on-Avon, Warwickshire, are found several such cottages as well as a maypole. Thomas Hardy was born in the thatched cottage (left) in Bockhampton, Dorset. Lyndhurst (facing page) is in Hampshire, as are the cottages (below).

The churches of England are perhaps her greatest treasure. They reflect the skill, faith and dedication of generations past. Upton Bishop (above) has a solidly built tower, which contrasts with that of Christchurch Priory (below), pierced as it is by the delicate window. The priory had its origins around the year 1100, as did the ruined castle, and displays a range of styles. Inside can be seen a monument to the poet Shelley and the splendid chantry chapels. (Left) the church at Marlow, Buckinghamshire and (facing page) Tewkesbury Abbey in Gloucestershire.

19

The cathedrals and churches of England have been witnesses to the dramas of history. St Mary's (facing page, top), Warwick, is famed as the church of the great Beauchamp Earls of Warwick. Richard Beauchamp was the benefactor of the beautiful fifteenth-century chapel which contains his tomb. Much of the church was rebuilt after a disastrous fire in 1694. Tewkesbury Abbey (top left and facing page, bottom) in Gloucestershire, witnessed the bloody defeat of the Lancastrian army of Queen Margaret at the hands of King Edward IV in 1471. Some of the fugitives fled to the Abbey for sanctuary. Ightham (bottom left) has only witnessed the unrecorded dramas of humbler lives and Guildford Cathedral (above) is barely half a century old.

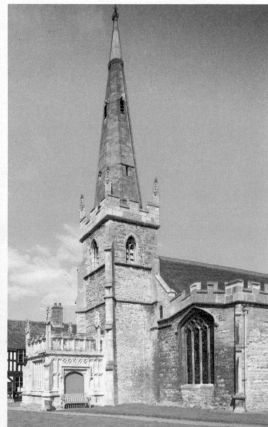

As the capital of the nation, London has a wealth of great buildings. Westminster Abbey (above) was founded by King Edward the Confessor in 1065, but was entirely rebuilt during the thirteenth and fourteenth centuries. The masterpiece of Sir Christopher Wren, St Paul's Cathedral (left) was begun in 1675. Buckingham Palace has its origins in a seventeenth-century mansion, but the familiar East Front (below) was not added until 1847. The Palace of Westminster (facing page) dates back to the reign of William II, but most of the building was rebuilt during the Victorian era, after a devastating fire.

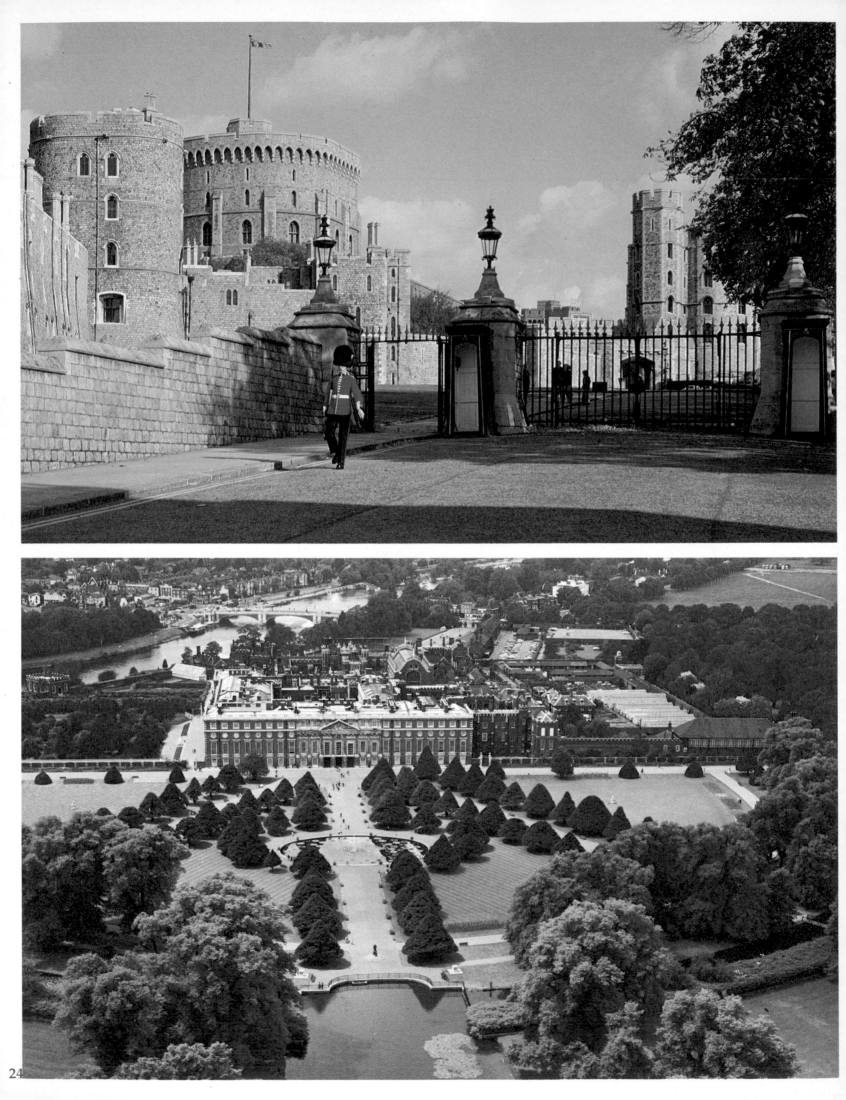

Sir Winston Churchill gazes resolutely down on Parliament Square (above). The gilded figure (right), that crowns the Victoria Memorial before Buckingham Palace, was unveiled in 1911. The Queen's House (bottom right), Greenwich, was designed by Inigo Jones for Queen Anne, wife of James I. Hampton Court (facing page, bottom) was built in two main phases, one Tudor and one Stuart. Windsor Castle (facing page, top) has been continually added to since it was built by William I. (Below) the Chinese Pagoda at Kew.

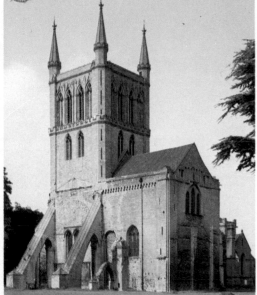

Many churches in England were once monastic foundations and suffered in the Dissolution. In Yorkshire the thirteenth-century Whitby Abbey (below) stands in ruins as does Bolton Abbey (top), a slightly older building. In York itself the remnants of St Mary's Abbey (right) date from the thirteenth century. Part of Pershore Abbey (above), Worcestershire, escaped the depredations of Henry VIII and became a parish church. Bath Abbey (above right) also survived. (Facing page) the West Front of York Minster.

Lymington, Hampshire, is famous for its Georgian houses (right) in Quay Hill. The Shambles (below) in York is a warren of narrow streets, as is the Lanes area of Brighton (facing page, centre right). Rye (top right), Sussex, was a major Channel port in the Middle Ages, its famous Mermaid Inn (facing page, top right) opened in 1420. Guildford, Surrey, is a bustling market town with the remarkable Guildhall (facing page, left) of 1683 in the cobbled High Street. (Above) Windsor, Berkshire.

Longleat (these pages) was built by Sir John Thynne in the 1570s, with the help of Robert Smythson. This Wiltshire mansion is often considered to be the finest Renaissance house in England. The palatial house was built to emphasise its horizontal lines, following the correct Classical usage of Doric on the ground floor, followed by Ionic and Corinthian above. Despite its Classical elegance and unity of construction, Longleat is very much an English house. Within its design it incorporates many features of the English country house that had developed during the Middle Ages. The symmetrically planned house is surrounded by superb grounds, which were landscaped by Capability Brown and now contain the famous safari park, complete with lions.

Oxford (these pages) has been a centre of learning for over eight hundred years, though the university dates from only 1214. Merton (above right) is one of the oldest colleges, founded in 1264. Oriel (right and below right) dates from 1324 and stands opposite the church of St Mary the Virgin. Oxford's Bridge of Sighs (above) is part of Hertford College. (Facing page): Nuffield College (bottom left) is one of the newest colleges. Magdalen (bottom right) is one of the wealthiest colleges and dates from the 15th century. St Edmund Hall (top) is now, after seven hundred years, a college. (Below) the Bodleian Library.

34

The churches and spires of London are notable landmarks of the capital. The Clock Tower of the Palace of Westminster (facing page and below) has become internationally known as a symbol of London. Inside the tower is the famous Big Ben, a thirteen-ton bell. Over the years the name has become attached to the clock itself. St Martin-in-the-Fields (right and above) overlooks Trafalgar Square. St Paul's (below right) still rises above the city, as it has done for three centuries.

(Above) Aberaeron, (below) Portmeirion and (right) the Dee near Llangollen.

A shepherd drives his sheep (above) in the Cader Idris mountains, which are wreathed in clouds (below left). (Below) the Coed-y-brenin forest.

37

Proudly announcing its title of "the smallest house in Great Britain", the building (far left) on Conway Quay certainly lives up to its name with two tiny rooms linked by a staircase. The tongue-twisting station sign (below) is now in the railway museum at Penrhyn Castle. The village name has been shortened to Llanfair P.G. It was as a coal exporting port that Barry (above) first gained prominence, but its sandy beach has turned it into a popular seaside resort. The little railways of Wales have become increasingly well known over the past few years. Ffestiniog Railway (below left) is one of the most popular, but the most dramatic must be the train (left) that climbs Snowdon.

LLANFAIRPWLLGWYNGYLLGOGERYCHWYRNDROBWYLL-LLANTYSILIOGOGOGOCH
RAILWAY STATION

At the Swallow Falls near Betws-y-coed the Llugwy, which means 'bright' in Welsh, tumbles through the gorge (left). After Edward I conquered North Wales in the thirteenth century he decided to hold onto his newly won lands with a string of powerful fortresses. Harlech (below) stands on a rocky crag to the south of Snowdonia, while Conway (above) guards the town of that name to the north of the mountains.

The island of Anglesey lies off the northwest coast of Wales, but is only separated from the mainland by the narrow Menai Straits. Today the straits are crossed by the Menai Straits Bridge (above). Built by Thomas Telford in 1826, it was the first suspension bridge of any size to be constructed and has survived to the present day as the only road bridge to the island. Beyond Anglesey stands Holy Island, where the lighthouse at South Stack (below) flashes its warning signal to shipping rounding the North Wales Coast. The beautiful Dee rushes over shallows near Llangollen (left).

Wales is a land of savage grandeur. The towering mountains of the principality have made it popular with climbers and walkers for years. To preserve the natural beauty of the land, some of its most outstanding areas have been set aside as National Parks. Snowdonia National Park (above and left) lies in Gwynedd and stretches from the north coast to beyond Cader Idris. Within its boundaries stands the highest land in Wales, and some of the most rugged, including Llanberis Pass (left). Further south the heights of Brecon Beacons National Park rise above the waters of Neuadd Reservoir (below).

The varied coast of Wales provides safe, sandy beaches, such as Tresaith (above) in Dyfed, and fine harbours for yachts and small craft, as at Conway (below). Further inland fertile valleys huddle beneath the bare hills, (left) at Craig Ddu in Powys.

48

Perhaps the most enduring image of Wales is its ruined vestiges of the Medieval period. Caernarvon Castle (above, above left, above far left and bottom centre) is one of the best preserved and most historic of these buildings. It was the site of a Roman fort and a manor of the native Princes of Gwynedd, but it was as an English town that it achieved greatness. After his conquest of North Wales in 1282 King Edward I built a series of mighty strongholds to maintain peace and order. Caernarvon is said to have been the birthplace of Edward II, first English Prince of Wales, and is now used as the setting for the Investiture of the Prince of Wales. Conway (left) was, like Caernarvon, an integrated town and castle complex built by royal command. Pembroke (centre, far left) and Cardiff (below), however, are baronial castles built over a period of time. (Bottom, far left) the ruins of Tintern Abbey in the Wye Valley.

49

Glasgow (above, left and above left) is the largest city in Scotland and is the heartland of Scottish industry. The city was founded in 543 by St Kentigern, also called St Mungo, when he built a church on the site. Further north the bustle of the big cities is lost in the fields of hay around Colla Firth (below) and the rushing waters of the River Dochart (far left).

Edinburgh (this page) is the capital of Scotland and has been the scene of human life since the Iron Age. It is crowded with historic buildings, each with a story to tell. Holyroodhouse (top left) was begun by James IV but is mainly the work of Charles II. It was in the private apartments of this palace that Rizzio, a favourite of Mary, Queen of Scots was brutally murdered in her presence in 1566. From Holyroodhouse the famous Royal Mile runs past John Knox's house (below) to the Castle (left). Knox was the ardent leader of the Reformation in Scotland and author of the *First Trumpet Blast against the Monstrous Regiment of Women*. In Princes Street Gardens, below the castle, stands the statue of Allan Ramsey (above). (Facing page) Ben Nevis rises above the waters of Loch Linnhe.

Scotland is a land with many faces. The tower (left) stands gaunt and tall above the River Tay. In St Andrews the Road Hole of the Old Course (below) is one of the finest belonging to the Royal and Ancient Golf Club. The Club was founded in 1754, but the course may well be three centuries older. This golf club, in a small town little known for anything else, is recognised as the world authority on the game. Perth (above and top) was the capital of Scotland for a century until, in 1437, James II moved his court to Edinburgh. The city has long been a beautiful and prosperous city and remains so today. It is famed for its livestock and seed potatoes, as well as whisky distilling and blending.

The magnificently sited castles of the Highlands (these pages) have long played a leading role in the history of the nation. Racked by clan feuds, rebellions and foreign invasion the castles remain gaunt witnesses to the past. Kilchurn Castle (above and facing page) stands on Loch Awe and Urquhart (below) on the monster-haunted Loch Ness. Eilean Donnan (right), however, stands at the strategic junction of Lochs Long, Duich and Alsh.

The many towns and villages that dot the coasts of Scotland and her islands have a long connection with fishing and the sea. Pittenweem (above, above left and below) is a small burgh on the Firth of Forth where fishing is still important in the economy. Mallaig (left) stands on the Sound of Sleat and is the end of the "Road to the Isles"; ferries leave its small harbour for Skye and thence the Western Isles. Scalloway (facing page, top) is a fishing port on the Shetlands and was once the capital of the islands. Today it is a quiet town, gathered around its ruined castle and fine harbour. Ayr (facing page, bottom) has been a royal burgh since 1203 and is famous for its links with Robert Burns. The poet was born just to the south and set many of his works in and around the town. The harbour is one of the busiest on the west coast.

Macbeth was Thane of Cawdor (left) before he killed King Duncan. (Above) Dunbeath Castle. Drummond Castle (below left) was built in 1491 and survived a bombardment during the Civil War. Abbotsford (below) was the home of Sir Walter Scott. Inveraray Castle (bottom left) is the home of the Duke of Argyll and for five hundred years has been the headquarters of the Clan Campbell. Blair Castle (bottom right) is the seat of the Duke of Atholl, who is the only man in Britain allowed to maintain a private army. (Facing page) Inverlochy Castle.

Founded in 1161, the cathedral of St Andrews was once the largest and most magnificent in Scotland, but following the famous sermon of John Knox at Perth the cathedral was sacked. Later generations took stone to build houses and the harbour, leaving the cathedral a mere ruin (below). Dundee (above) is a beautiful city but is perhaps most famous for its two extremely long bridges (left). The Tay Rail Bridge was built in 1887 to replace the earlier bridge that collapsed in 1879 killing 75 people. Next to it is the Tay Road Bridge, built in 1966.

Killin (right) is a year round holiday resort near Loch Tay. People flock here to enjoy the fishing, boating or to tramp the hills around nearby Tyndrum (above right). Dotted around Scotland are many kinds of castle. Some are forbidding medieval fortresses of great strength, Stirling (above) exemplifying the type. For over 800 years the crag has been fortified and has seen many a siege. In 1314 the castle was held by the English against Robert the Bruce. An attempt by the English to relieve the castle resulted in the Battle of Bannockburn, just to the south. Extensive rebuilding in the fifteenth century transformed the castle into a palace. Culzean Castle (top) was built by Robert Adam in 1777 as a comfortable mansion around an earlier stronghold. Balmoral (facing page) only dates from 1853, when Prince Albert designed it, in the Scottish Baronial style, as a Highland retreat for himself and Queen Victoria. It has remained a Royal dwelling ever since and is the venue for an annual holiday by the Queen.

On a promontory that was once an island in Loch Awe (left) stands the ruin of Kilchurn Castle (above). Originally built in 1440 by Colin Campbell, the castle was added to in the 1690s by the Earl of Breadalbane. Loch Long (below left) is dominated by Ben Arthur, a 2,891-foot peak. Its calm waters have also witnessed the raids of Vikings. The solitary tower (below) in the heart of windswept Glenfinnan, marks the spot where Bonnie Prince Charlie unfurled his banner and called the clans to arms in 1745. The impressive monument was built on the orders of Macdonald of Glenaladale in 1815 and is topped by a statue of a highlander. One of the most beautiful and impressive of all glens in Scotland is Glencoe (facing page). It was in these dramatic surroundings that soldiers led by a Campbell fell upon the Macdonalds and slaughtered them in their beds. Every village in the glen was burned and many more Macdonalds died of exposure that winter.